PLAYING WITH
PLASTICINE

PLAYING WITH
PLASTICINE
BARBARA REID

MORROW JUNIOR BOOKS/NEW YORK

Plasticine® is the registered Trade Mark used exclusively for modeling materials manufactured in England by Peter Pan Playthings Limited, Bretton Way, Bretton, Peterborough PE3 8YA, and distributed in the United States by Peter Pan Playthings Inc. of 200 Fifth Avenue, New York, N.Y. 10016.

Printed in the United States of America.
1 2 3 4 5 6 7 8 9 10

Library of Congress Cataloging-in-Publication Data
Reid, Barbara,
    Playing with plasticine / Barbara Reid.
        p. cm.
        Summary: Instructions for turning the modeling material known as
    Plasticine (or a similar modeling clay) into flat picures and three-
    dimensional objects.
        ISBN 0-688-08415-X (lib. bdg.). ISBN 0-688-08414-1 (pbk.)
        1. Modeling.   2. Art—Study and teaching (Elementary)
    [1. Modeling.   2. Handicraft.]   I. Title.
    N350.R45   1988
    745.5—dc 19   88-39564   CIP   AC

Contents

Playing with Plasticine

If you've ever picked up a piece of Plasticine, you'll know how easy it is to squish and roll around in your hands. You'll also know how difficult it is to put down once you've started playing with it.

Plasticine was invented about 100 years ago. Ever since then, people have been kneading it into every shape under the sun. Sculptors sometimes use it to make a model of something that will later be cast in metal. Maybe you've seen television cartoons with animated Plasticine figures.

The best thing about Plasticine (besides the feel) is that it never gets hard. You could shape a piece of Plasticine into something different every day for a whole *year* and you'd still be able to make it into even more things. If you forgot about it for a whole year and then found it at the back of a drawer, it would just take two warm hands and a few squeezes and pinches to get it back into working order. (But really — how could you forget about Plasticine once you discovered what neat stuff it is!)

This book has a lot of ideas for making things out of Plasticine. It starts with simple shapes and goes on to combine them to make more detailed figures and pictures. These are only ideas and suggestions, not rules. Plasticine is made to bend and change, so feel free to bend and change these ideas to make your own creations. A lump of Plasticine and an imagination are the ingredients for many hours of fun.

ALL ABOUT PLASTICINE

Plasticine is available in 1-pound bars of single colours and in smaller packs of several colours. It can be found in art and craft supply stores and some toy stores.

Plasticine is oily, so don't use it on a surface it can damage. A hard, smooth surface is the best. Kitchen tables are very good, but are sometimes off limits. The shiny smooth side of a big piece of Masonite board is an excellent surface and, best of all, can be moved around (even onto the kitchen table, if you get a chance). Another good surface is a smooth piece of illustration board (a type of stiff cardboard sold at art supply stores). In this book, we'll call the hard surface *the board*.

No matter how careful you are, some Plasticine will fall on the floor. Pick it up right away, because it NEVER comes off the rug once someone steps on it.

SOME USEFUL TOOLS FOR PLASTICINE PLAY

A knife: Plasticine is very soft so you don't need a sharp knife. Even a nail file or the edge of a ruler will work. You'll use a knife for cutting some shapes, and it's also handy for scraping a surface clean.

Round pencils: The point of a pencil can be used to make many kinds of textures and dots. A round pencil can also be used as a roller, to flatten objects.

Wires, paper clips, toothpicks: These are handy for cutting, poking and prodding the Plasticine into the shapes you want.

Tools for special effects: Such things as combs, garlic presses, tooth brushes and bits of textured cloth can give some really neat effects. Make sure it's okay with the owner before you use them (sometimes the Plasticine is hard to get off things). Try to find things that no one is using any more.

Your hands!: These are probably the most useful tools. They help warm up the Plasticine and make it easier to use and pinch and roll most of the shapes. Fingernails can cut Plasticine and make little curving lines and textures on the surface.

Above all, use your imagination and you'll find all sorts of objects that can become part of your Plasticine tool bag.

STORAGE TIPS

Plasticine never gets hard, but it often gets dirty. Small bits of fuzz, lint, dog and cat hairs and cookie crumbs will stick to your Plasticine. If too many things get into Plasticine, it's not very nice to work with. So when you're not using it, store your Plasticine in plastic yogurt or margarine tubs. It will stay clean so you can use it over and over. And you can keep the colours separate, too.

ABOUT COLOUR

Plasticine is available in many colours. You can make even more colours by mixing it. For example, take a piece of red and a piece of white Plasticine. Squish and knead the two pieces together over and over until you get one smooth colour — pink! Different combinations will make other colours. For example:

Blue and yellow = green
Red and yellow = orange
Red and blue = purple

More of one colour than another will result in, say, a more reddish purple or a more bluish green. Experiment and invent your own colours and shades.

After a while, you may have a lot of colours that have become stuck together. They'll never come apart. Sometimes this looks very interesting, like marble. If you'd rather have a solid colour, mix all the bits together. It may take a long time, but you'll end up with a ball of all one colour. Most likely it will be a dull greyish-brown, but it depends on what has gone into it.

If you keep Plasticine clean, it can be used many times, and the occasional new package will help build your colour collection.

BASIC SHAPES

When you begin to make something out of Plasticine, start small. A great big lump of Plasticine is often too hard to mould.

The very first thing to do with a piece of Plasticine is to warm it up by rolling and kneading it for a few minutes. The Plasticine will get soft and smooth, and your fingers will be in the mood to work with it. Soften up more Plasticine a bit at a time and add to it as you make things.

By practicing the basic shapes below, you'll get an idea of what Plasticine can do. And these shapes will help make almost anything you can imagine. The best part is, if what you're making doesn't work quite the way you want, you can squash it up and try again.

Ball

Form a rough ball with your fingers and then roll it round and round between your palms. The more you roll it, the smoother and rounder the ball will become. Try making balls of different sizes.

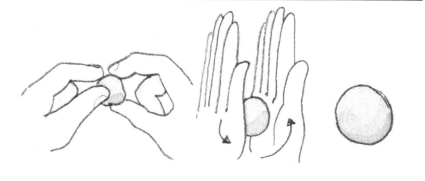

Egg

Start with a round ball. Instead of rolling it around with your palms, gently roll it up and down. When it has become a longer oval shape, use your fingers to round the ends to form a smooth egg.

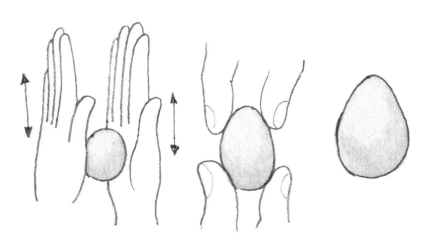

10

Pancake

You can make a pancake from a ball. Just pinch the ball between your finger and thumb and flatten it out. If the edge of the pancake cracks, smooth the cracks over with your fingers. Pancakes can be made in many sizes and thicknesses.

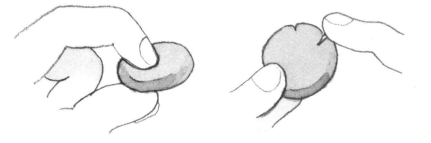

Drop

To make a drop shape, pinch one side of a ball into a point. Keep turning the round shape in your fingers and pinching the point until the Plasticine looks like a nice fat drop of water.

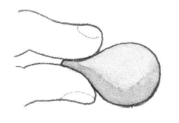

Teepee

By pressing the big end of a drop onto your board, it gets a flat bottom and becomes a miniature teepee.

Snake

One of the most useful shapes is a snake. Roll a piece of Plasticine back and forth on the board until it gets long and thin. The more you roll it, the longer and thinner it will become. With practice, your snake can become very smooth and even. Very thin snakes sometimes break but can be easily stuck back together and rolled again.

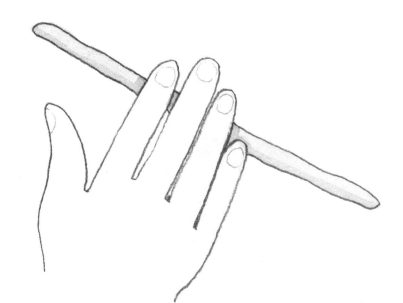

Sausage

A sausage is just a short, thick snake.

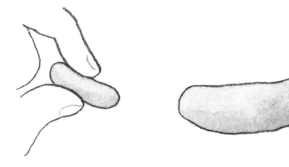

Cylinder

To make a cylinder shape, roll out a short fat sausage and press each end flat on the board. Once the ends are flat you may need to roll it again to round it out. Cutting the ends of the sausage with a knife is another way to make a cylinder shape.

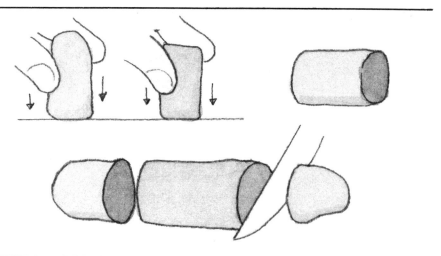

Box

Starting with a cylinder, you can make a box. Place a short cylinder on its side and gently press it with another small smooth board (or the lid of a jar, the bottom of a cup or anything flat). Roll it over so that the flat top is on the side. Press it again. The cylinder now has four sides. Stand the box on end and press again. Now it should look like a box. By turning and pressing the box on different sides you can make many shapes and sizes of boxes.

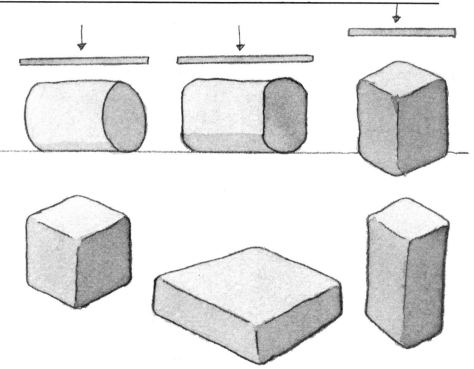

Ribbon

To make a flat ribbon, begin with a snake about the size of a pencil. Lay the snake on the board and roll a pencil back and forth over it. The pencil becomes a mini-steamroller and flattens the snake into a ribbon of Plasticine. The tricky part is carefully peeling the ribbon from the board so that it can be used to make something. It might take a bit of practice to flatten the ribbon without sticking it to the board. A smooth shiny work surface helps, and don't try and make the ribbon too thin.

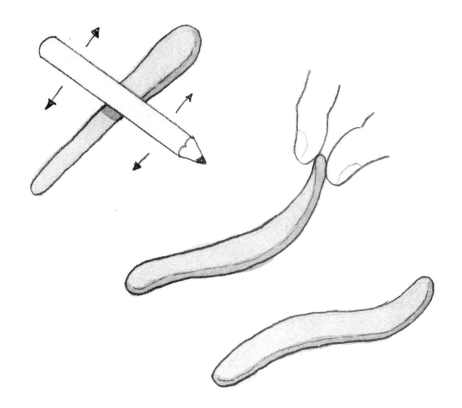

Of course there are lots of other shapes that can be made with Plasticine, but these will get you going. Start playing!

1. Bugs, Birds and Beasts

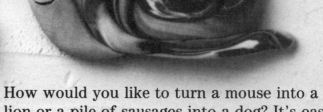

How would you like to turn a mouse into a lion or a pile of sausages into a dog? It's easy with Plasticine.

This chapter starts out with simple animal shapes and then gives you suggestions to turn them into a whole zoofull of creatures. You don't have to go through this chapter in order — a suggestion on one page might combine with one a few pages later to help make what you have in mind. So let your imagination run wild and, most importantly, have fun.

TIPS

When you have to stick two parts together, such as a leg to a body, press *firmly* so that they won't fall apart later. You might have to reshape the figure afterwards, but it's good to attach things solidly.

To make an invisible joint, gently smooth the Plasticine with your finger so that the joint is covered. Pat it flat. Blending two pieces together in this way makes the joint stronger, too.

Snakes and Snails

Take a simple shape (the snake) and turn it into something s-s-s-super.

1 Roll out — you guessed it — a snake shape. At one end, roll it into a point to form the tail.

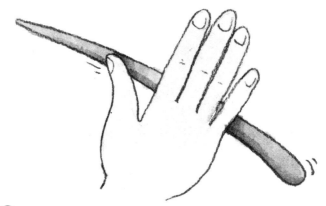

2 Roll out a smaller, thin snake for a tongue. To make a forked tongue, fold this piece in half. Leave the ends spread apart and pinch and roll the folded part smooth.

3 Attach the tongue to the bottom of the snake's head. Make two small balls for eyes and press them onto the head.

4 Draw on a mouth with the point of a pencil. Presto — your snake is done!

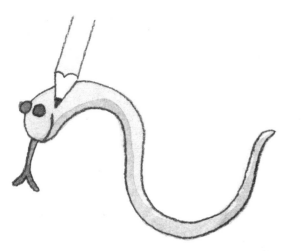

5 This snake can curl into many positions. It can also be decorated with spots by pressing some small pancake shapes onto it.

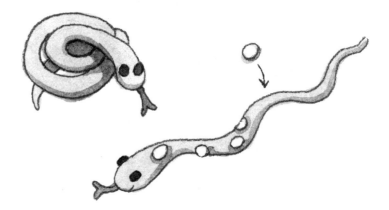

6 To make a striped snake, start with two snake shapes of different colours. Put them side by side and pinch together at the top. Start at the top and twist them together. Roll the twisted piece smooth and you have a striped snake!

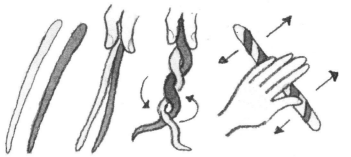

7 Experiment with different thicknesses of stripes or try using more than two colours. This striped snake can also become a candy cane, a barber's pole or ....

8 To turn a snake into a snail, roll it up like a rug, starting at the thin end. Leave a little bit sticking out the end and stand it up, pressing it onto the board to flatten the bottom.

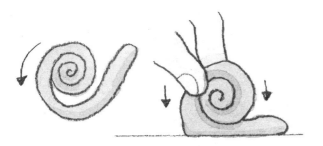

9 Add some eyes to the sticking-out-bit (it's the head). Instead of a snake tongue, give the snail some feelers. Attach a small tail onto the back.

10 Snails made from striped snakes in many colours can be very pretty. Like real snails they can stick to a smooth wall or glass. But be careful where you stick your snail. Plasticine is oily and it can leave marks.

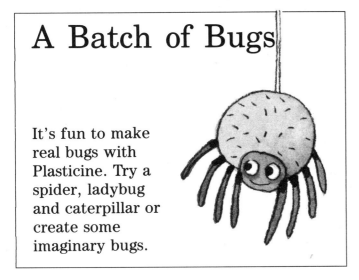

A Batch of Bugs

It's fun to make real bugs with Plasticine. Try a spider, ladybug and caterpillar or create some imaginary bugs.

1 To make a spider, start with a ball of Plasticine. Lightly press it onto the board to give it a flat bottom.

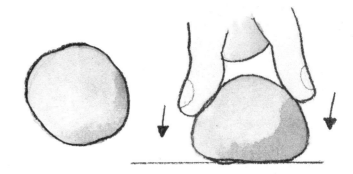

2 While the ball is still on the board, stick a smaller ball on for a head. Add some googly eyes.

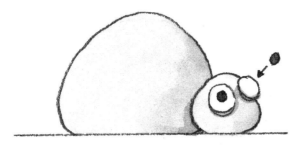

3 Roll out eight thin snakes for legs. Pick up the spider and attach them onto its flat bottom. Your spider is done.

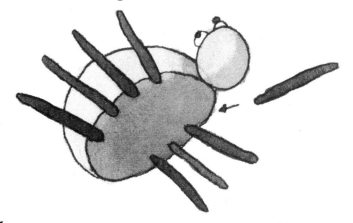

4 For a ladybug, make two eggs the same size. Press them together and pinch the tops and bottoms to make a round shape that's split down the middle. This is your ladybug's shell.

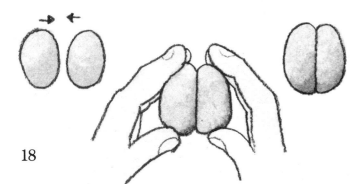

5 Press the shell onto the table and add a head, just as you did for the spider. Press on six legs and two feelers, plus some round spots.

6 A caterpillar also starts with a ball. Stick another ball the same size onto it. Then add another, and another and so on. When it's long enough, add a larger ball for a head.

7 Legs can be made by attaching a thin snake across the bottom of each ball (except the head) so that a bit sticks out each side.

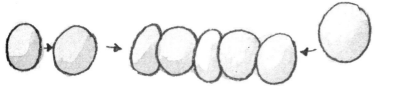

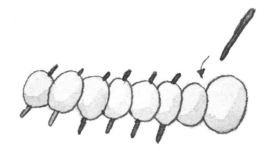

8 Press dots into the head with a sharp pencil to make eyes. To make a mouth, press your thumb or fingernail into the Plasticine. Curving up, it's a smile, curving down it's a frown.

9 Using spider, ladybug and caterpillar shapes you can come up with all sorts of weird and wonderful bugs. Dot them, stripe them and experiment with their shapes. One idea is to use the snail shape from page 17 to make curving feelers. How about adding wings?

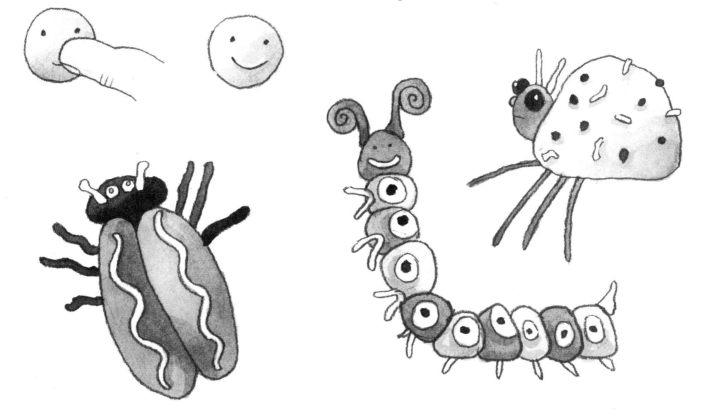

A Simple Seal and Sidekick

The smooth shape and flexible body of a seal is perfect for Plasticine. Make a few changes and you can turn it into another sea creature — the walrus!

1 Start with a big drop shape and pinch the round end into a point.

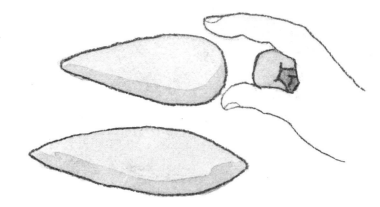

2 Lay the pinched drop on the board. Bend one end up and forward so that you have an S shape.

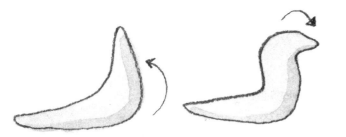

3 Give your seal some tail flippers by carefully splitting the tail end in two with a knife or wire.

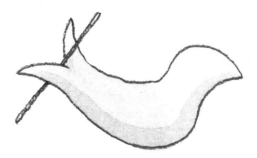

4 Spread the tail flippers apart and pinch them flat. Add two flipper-shaped triangles to the front of the seal, at the body bend. The points of the flippers should touch the board.

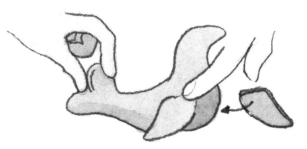

5 To make an open mouth, cut into the pointed part of the head with a knife. Open the mouth slightly with your fingers.

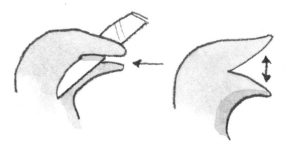

6 With a sharp pencil, dot in some eye holes. Add a round ball for a nose. Now your seal is ready to do some tricks.

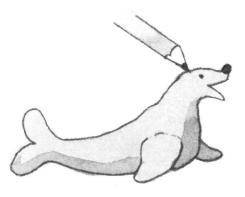

7 A seal can curve and twist into many positions. Make some boxes or cylinders for it to play on or a ball to balance on its nose.

8 To make a walrus, press the nose into a flat, stubby snout. Roll some small pointed sausages and stick them on, pointing down.

9 With a sharp pencil, dot in eyes and draw on some whiskers. Add a ball nose.

Leapin' Lizards

Whether they're shelled, scaly, spiny or slippery, reptiles are great to make out of Plasticine.

1 To make a turtle, start with a thick pancake body for the bottom shell. Add four sausage legs, a bigger sausage head and a small sausage tail.

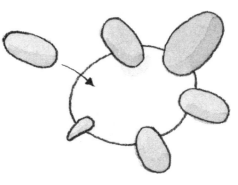

2 Make another slightly bigger pancake for the top shell. Press it over the bottom shell, so that it's slightly rounded.

3 Use a sharp pencil to dot in some eyes and add texture to its shell.

4 To make a crocodile, roll a thick snake with a pointed tail.

5 Carefully cut the head end with a knife or wire. This mouth opening should take up about one-third of the body.

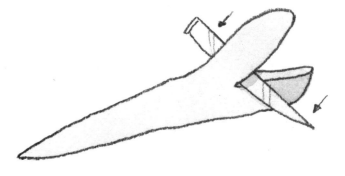

6 Stick two small balls on the end of the snout and dot them with a pencil for nostrils. Add two bigger balls on the head for eyes. Starting at the back of the mouth, add some teepee-shaped teeth.

7 Four sausages become legs. Add some pointy claws. Bend the croc's body and tail into whatever position you want.

8 To make scales, start at one end and press on a row of small pancakes. Add a second row so that it just overlaps the first. Keep overlapping row by row until the area you want to be scaly is covered.

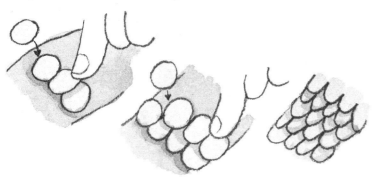

9 Drawing some squiggly lines down a reptile's back with a sharp pencil is another way to make a texture.

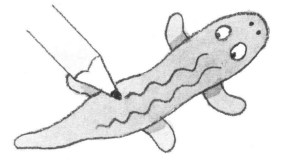

10 Lizards come in hundreds of shapes. Combine scales and spikes with different head and tail shapes and invent a whole world of reptiles. And remember — dragons are reptiles, too!

Birds of a Feather

Start with a basic bird and create a whole flock of fabulous flyers by adding different kinds of feathers, wings, tails and beaks.

1 To make a bird's body, press a drop shape onto the board to give it a flat bottom. Tip it slightly so that the pointed end (the tail) is up. Add a ball for the head.

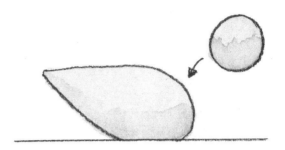

2 Make two smaller drops and flatten them. Press these wings onto the sides of the bird's body.

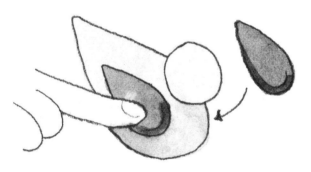

3 Make a beak by sticking a teepee shape onto the head. The beak can be short or long, fat or thin, curved or straight. Dot on some eyes.

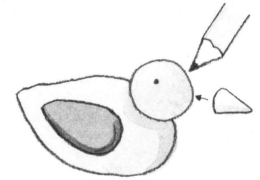

4 Press flattened sausage shapes onto the tail for fancy tail feathers. Add two small balls for feet.

5 To turn the basic bird shape into a duck, make a duck bill by pressing two flat ovals together and attaching them to the bird's head.

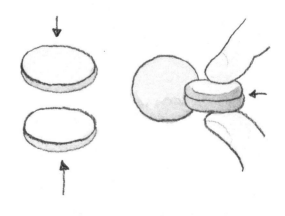

6 A duck's flat webbed feet can be made from two flattened triangles. Don't forget to turn up the duck's tail — ducks like to wag their tails.

7 A duck can become a goose by adding a longer neck. Attach a short snake for a neck, but be sure it's thick enough to support the head.

8 Swans have smaller bills than ducks and long, curving necks. Their wings are bigger and point up, over the back.

9 If you leave the feet off ducks, geese and swans and put them on a mirror, you can create a duck pond. You can even add some "odd birds" if you wish.

Sitting Pretty

Begin by making a sitting cat, then try other animal "sitters."

1 Roll out an egg shape and press the bigger end onto the board so that it stands up.

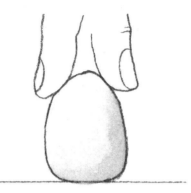

2 Attach a pancake to the bottom half of each side of the egg.

3 Make back legs by adding a small sausage to the bottom of each pancake. Add two longer sausages to the front of the body about three-quarters of the way up. These are the front legs.

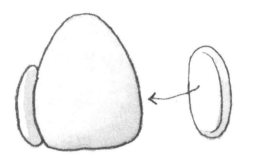

4 Add a round ball to the top of the egg for a head. To make ears, make two small drop shapes and press them onto each side of the head.

5 Press two small pancakes together onto the bottom half of the cat's face for a muzzle. Add a small ball to the bottom of the muzzle for a chin, and another to the top of the muzzle for a nose.

6 Cats' eyes can be made by attaching two ovals to the face. Draw a short line down each oval with a sharp pencil to make the pupil and draw on some whiskers.

7 Add a tail and your cat is done. You can turn the cat's head or add a tongue. Add some thin snake shapes and your cat is striped.

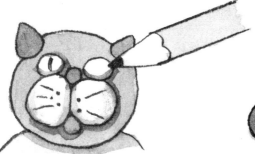

8 What would happen to the cat if it grew a mane and a tassel on the end of its tail?

9 Change a cat into a mouse. Instead of a round head, use a drop shape and put a little mouse nose at the end. Two pancakes become ears. The front paws are small and tucked up. Draw on eyes and whiskers.

10 Play around with different sorts of heads and tails to make a rabbit, squirrel, beaver or kangaroo.

27

Standing Animals

Start by making a sausage dog out of a sausage shape, then put some other animals on their feet.

1 Roll one large sausage for the body and four smaller sausages for legs. Lay the body on the board and stick on the smaller sausages.

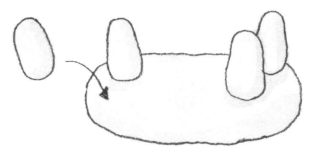

2 Turn the whole thing over and gently press down to make the legs even. You might have to wiggle it around a bit to make it steady. Add a small sausage tail.

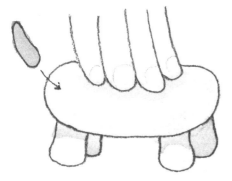

3 Add a round ball on top of the other end for a head. Make a stubby cylinder and add it to the front of the head for a snout.

4 Carefully cut the snout through the middle with a wire or knife. Open this mouth carefully with your fingers. Stick a small ball on for a nose and add a tiny sausage tongue.

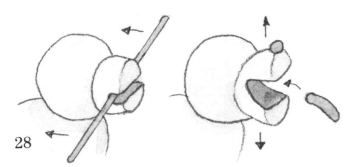

5 Add one flattened triangle to each side of the head for ears. Attach two small balls for eyes and dot in the pupils with a sharp pencil.

6 With different body, ear, tail and snout shapes, you can make all sorts of dogs. Cover your dog with mini-pancakes and call your pet Spot. Or make it look furry by scratching on some lines with a sharp pencil. Try to get the dog to lie down, roll over or sit up. If it's good, give it a bone.

7 If you use a drop shape for a head, pointed ears and a very fat drop shape for a tail, a dog will become one of its cousins — a fox.

8 To make a raccoon, start with a short, fat body, a pointed head and two dark pancakes where the eyes will go. This is the raccoon's mask. Add balls for eyes on top of the mask.

9 Build a striped tail by stacking pancakes of two different colours. Top it off with a teepee. Press the layers together firmly and put the tail on its side to roll the edges smooth. Pinch it into a nice bushy tail shape.

A Zoofull of Animals

Let your imagination go wild and make a whole zoofull of animals. Just remember that the bigger the body, the sturdier the legs must be.

1 To make a bear, start with an egg shape and add four thick cylinder legs. What kind of tail should you make?

2 Add a ball head at the front of the body and make a snout like a dog's (see step 3, page 28). Add small half-pancake ears and dot in the eyes with a sharp pencil.

3 By moving the bear's legs apart, changing its head position and flattening its bottom, it can sit up.

4 To make a pig, start with a fat egg, add four sausage legs, a cylinder snout with nostril holes, ball eyes and a curly tail.

5 The pig's ears can be made by pinching one side of a small pancake. Press the pinched part onto the head. Or use a pencil to poke them in place so that they don't get squashed.

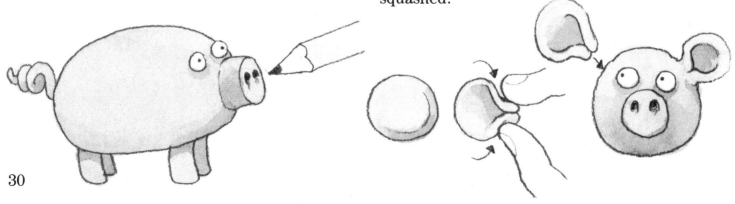

6 Horses, zebras and giraffes all have long, thin legs. To help them stand up, **make the feet big** or try sticking the two front legs and two back legs together. If all else fails, make two animals and lean them together.

7 Thick-legged elephants stand easily. To make smooth elephant (or any other animal) legs quickly, roll a long snake and cut it into four pieces of equal length.

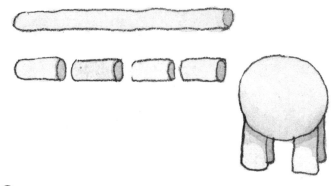

8 To make an elephant head and trunk, roll a ball and pinch a bit of it between your fingers. Roll and pull this trunk until it's the right length. The nostrils go at the end.

9 Some big pancake ears, two small sausage tusks and a tiny tail and your elephant is finished.

10 Try making some farm animals or play around with animal positions. You could even combine parts of different animals to create a new animal. Hmmmm... now what would a gir-ouse-ephant look like? A rabb-opotamus?

2. Body Building

A clown, a pirate, an Olympic athlete or yourself — you can make all sorts of people with Plasticine. The suggestions in this chapter will get you started building lots of bodies.

TIPS

Because people have only two legs instead of four, it's often more difficult to get Plasticine people to stand up. Once you've finished a figure, try gently inserting a piece of toothpick up each leg to stiffen it. Make sure the toothpick isn't too long or it may poke out the top! As with animals, thicker legs and longer feet will also help your figures stand. Or you can prop them up against chairs and other objects from Part 3. Try sitting (or lying) them down. If nothing else works, make a Plasticine base for your figure. A base will also prevent a figure from getting damaged when you move it around.

Basic Body Building

Plasticine people can be simple or very detailed. Two simple ''people'' to start with are a snowman and a robot. Then try building the real thing.

1 A Plasticine snowman is built just like a real one, but use toothpicks for arms, a mini-Plasticine carrot for a nose and a ribbon shape for a scarf. A cylinder on top of a pancake makes a great top hat.

2 To make a robot, put together a box body and head and some cylinders. Make bolts with small pencil dots or tiny balls. Add any texture you want.

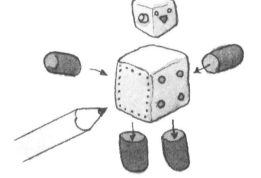

3 To make a basic human, begin with a short, fat cylinder body. Flatten it slightly so that you have a back and a front.

4 Roll a snake and fold it in half for legs. Press the fold onto the body. Turn the ends of the legs up a bit to form feet.

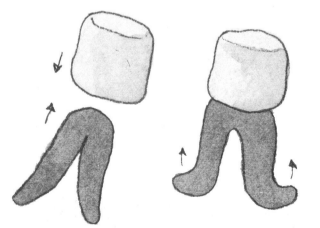

5 To stand the figure up, hold onto the legs and feet and press the figure onto the board. If your figure wobbles, try thicker legs or shorter ones or stick the legs together.

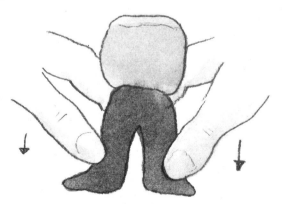

6 Arms can be made from two sausages attached at the shoulder. A round ball on top becomes a head.

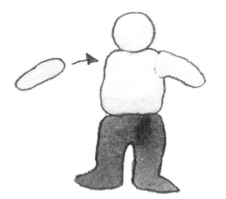

7 To make hands, start with a small ball and pinch out a thin thumb of Plasticine. Roll this thumb as you pinch it. Flatten the hand part into a pancake and bend the thumb alongside the palm.

8 This mitten-like hand can be attached to the arms. You can even cut fingers into it with a knife.

9 Poke in eyes with a sharp pencil, add a tiny ball nose and press in a fingernail smile.

10 The basic person can do many things. It is also the start of hundreds of different Plasticine people. For some ideas, turn the page.

35

People Parts

People come in many shapes and sizes, and their clothes change the way they look. Here are some ideas to try out on the basic person you made on page 35.

Skirts. Use a drop shape or an egg to make a skirt. A long skirt will help your person stand up.

Shorter skirts. Make a large thin pancake and shape it over your finger. Push the legs up under it. This shape can also form a cape or a hat.

Ballet tutu. Attach a thick pancake to the body before you add on the legs. Make it frilly by pressing a wire into the edge all the way around.

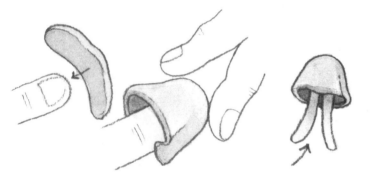

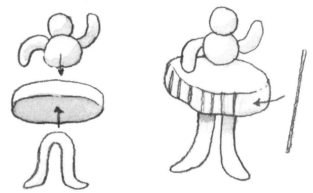

Shorts. Bend a short snake in half and flatten the ends. Stick on legs — long thin ones or short thick ones.

Footwear. Your people can wear tall boots or flat triangle flippers. Elves might wear slippers with curled-up toes that have a bell on the end.

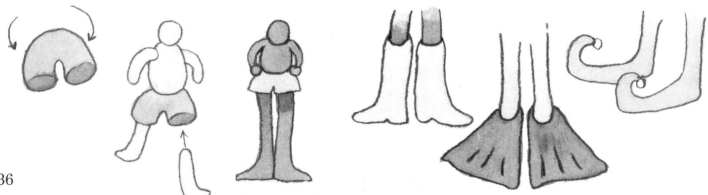

Collars and scarves. Add a pancake collar between the head and body or wrap your person up with a snake or ribbon scarf.

Hats. Combine teepees, cylinders, pancakes and eggs to make a bunch of hats.

Finishing touches. Don't forget buttons, bows and belts. And you can make polka dots out of small pancakes or draw on plaids or stripes with a sharp pencil.

For some real fun, try making clowns — they have interesting body shapes and clothes. Or experiment with other circus characters or your own favourites, like witches, Vikings or princesses.

Face It!

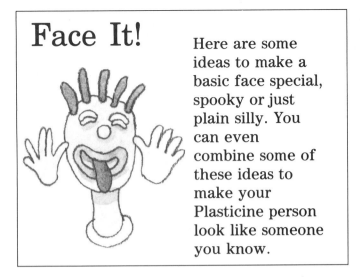

Here are some ideas to make a basic face special, spooky or just plain silly. You can even combine some of these ideas to make your Plasticine person look like someone you know.

Ears. Make a small sausage and curve it into a C shape. Press it onto the head. What if you're making a Martian with big pointed ears? Experiment!

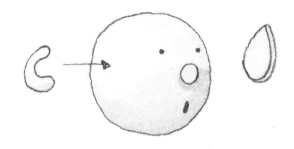

Eyes. Poke eye holes with a sharp pencil. Or try a small ball with a pencil dot or another smaller ball as a pupil. These eyes can look in any direction. Add on eyebrows and eyelashes.

Mouths. A basic mouth can be made by pressing your fingernail into the Plasticine. Add lips made out of thin snakes. These snake lips can give many expressions. To make Dracula, add pointy fangs.

Open mouths. Use a knife to carve into the head. Cut a slice out to make the mouth wide open. The deeper the cut, the bigger the mouth. A flat sausage makes a good tongue.

Noses. Press a teepee-shaped nose onto the head and poke in nostrils with a sharp pencil. Now play around with other noses — long ones, curved ones, fat ones and turned up ones.

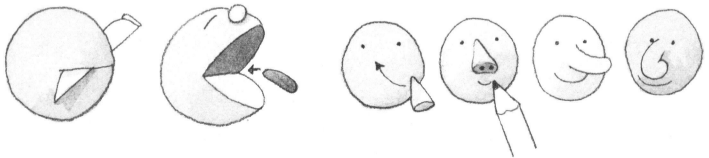

Necks and heads. Use a cylinder to make a neck. Lots of shapes can be used for heads, including eggs, balls and drops. Cheeks can be made with small pancakes. And don't forget about freckles.

Hairstyles. Wrap a big, thin pancake over a head. Add some sausage pigtails.

Cover a head with long, thin snakes. Braid them if you wish.

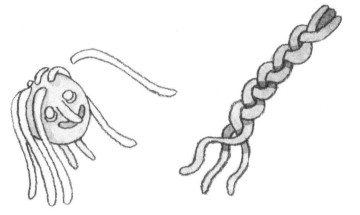

For a wild look, try some spikes. Curly hair can be made with coiled snakes or with cylinders or round balls.

Mix ideas and invent your own hairstyles.

39

3. A Whole Bunch of Stuff

You can make everything from fruit bowls to furniture to fast cars using the ideas in this chapter. These objects can stand alone or they can be props for Plasticine people.

TIPS

When building large objects or adding one object to another, use a strong, heavy Plasticine base so that things don't tip over. Inserting a toothpick will sometimes steady things too. If the main body of an object is made from one big solid chunk of Plasticine, the object will hold together better than if it is made of a bunch of little pieces.

Stuff in a Basket

Want to make baskets or pots that you can put things into? Here's how, plus some ideas for stuff to go in them.

1 To make a basket, start with a thick pancake for the bottom. Roll a long thin snake and coil it around the edge of the pancake. Keep coiling until your basket is as high as you want.

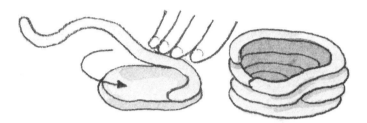

2 Pinch the sides so that the coils stick together. You can also slightly change the shape of the basket. Use a small snake as a handle.

3 To give the basket a fancy woven look, twist two thin snakes together (see step 6, page 17), then wind the coils around and around as you did before.

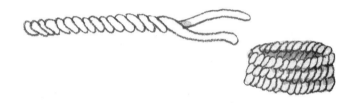

4 Make fruit for your basket out of balls and sausage shapes. How would you make a pineapple?

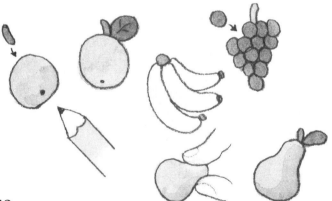

5 To make an ear of corn, start with a sausage and draw criss-cross lines on it. Use three or four thin, flat sausages to make the leaves. Now try peas in a pod.

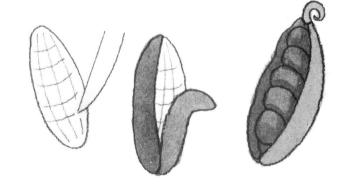

6 Pumpkins are fun to make. Start with a round ball and press a flat sausage onto it, going from top to bottom. Keep adding sausages all the way around. Stick a stem on top.

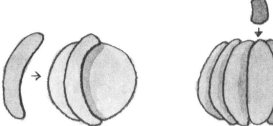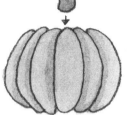

7 Put your pumpkin and other fruits and vegetables into a wide-bottomed Thanksgiving basket.

8 To make a basket filled with balls of wool, start by rolling out lots of thin snakes. Roll the snakes up like balls of wool, put the balls in a basket and add some knitting needles.

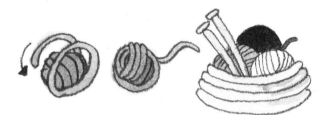

9 Now try a basket of eggs or a bird's nest.

10 Your basket could have a pancake lid that covers up what's inside.

Do the Dishes

Tea-time wouldn't be much fun for Plasticine people without teapots or cups. Here's how to make them and maybe even a dish for the dog, too.

1 To make a bowl or cup, press a ball over your finger (or other smooth, rounded object) and pinch and turn it. Carefully take your finger out and press the bottom on the board to flatten it.

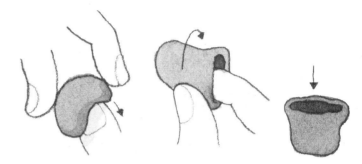

2 Another way to make a bowl is to use the coil method (see step 1, page 42) and smooth the coils flat when you're done.

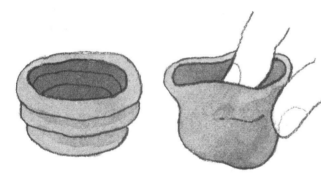

3 Handles can be made by pressing curved sausages onto the sides and smoothing them into place.

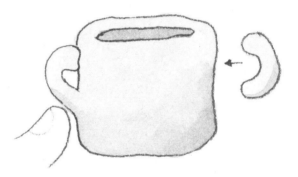

4 Make plates from different sizes of pancakes. You can finish them off with a thin snake around the edge.

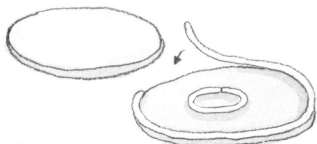

5 Roll out three short snakes. Flatten half of one to make a knife. Flatten the end of one and make three cuts for a fork. Add a curved pancake to one to make a spoon.

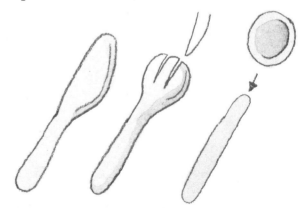

6 To make an egg-cup or fancy bowl, use a teepee or pyramid for the base. Then stick on a bowl.

7 To make a teapot, start with a ball or egg shape and add a spout, handle and lid.

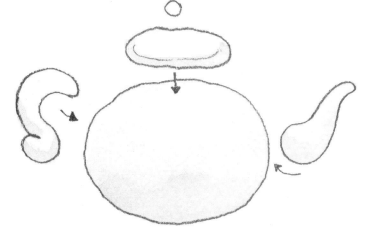

8 Experiment with handles, lids and decorations to make all kinds of dishes. Add some Plasticine food and serve your favourite meal.

Fun with Furniture

Plasticine people and animals sometimes want to sit down or take a nap or eat dinner. Here are some ways to make them comfortable.

1 The simplest chair is a three-legged stool. Attach three sausages to a pancake. Turn the stool over and press gently until it's steady.

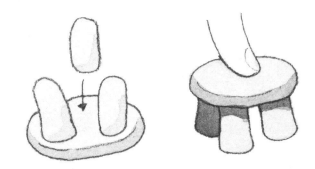

2 You can make many stool variations. Try using four legs or a more modern drop-shaped base. Make longer legs and your stool becomes a table.

3 To make a chair with a back, flatten an egg shape into a pancake and bend it. Add the legs as you did for the stool.

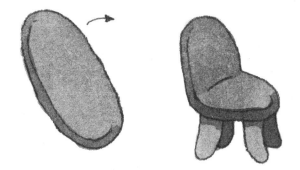

4 Attaching a curved snake to the stool will make a back too. As long as the seat and legs of the chair are heavier than the back, it will stand up.

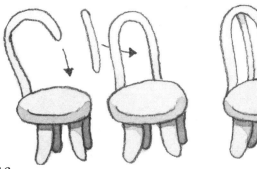

5 A cosy armchair is fun to make. Start with a flat box shape. Add another one the same size. This is your chair base.

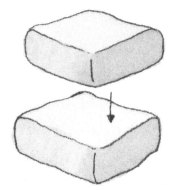

6 Stand a nice thick pancake up to make the back. Two thick cylinders form the arms and join the back and seat.

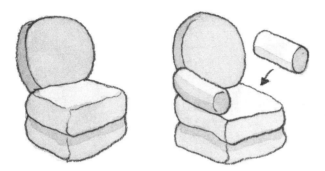

7 A very wide armchair is a sofa. Add some cushions and buttons if you like.

8 By adding some posts made of sausages and some pillows, a box becomes a bed.

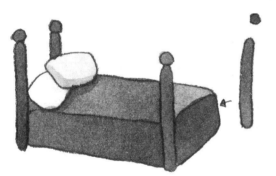

9 To make lamps, put a bowl shape (see steps 1 and 2, page 44) on top of a base. Try different styles of lamps.

10 Look around your house to see what kinds of furniture you can make. Remember — if you are adding people or animals, the heavier they are, the stronger the furniture legs must be. An elephant can't sit on a piano stool!

Get Rolling!

Hidden inside a blob of Plasticine is a whole fleet of fast-moving toys and vehicles.

1 Curl up the end of a fat ribbon to make a toboggan — or a flying carpet.

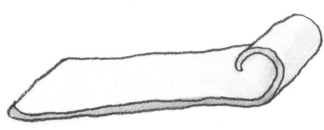

2 Pinch a flat sausage into a skateboard shape and add two cylinders. Turn up the end and get ready to roll.

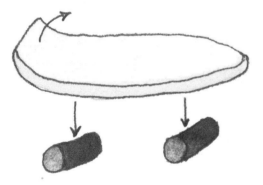

3 To make a car, start with a long box for the body. Stick a smaller box on top for a roof.

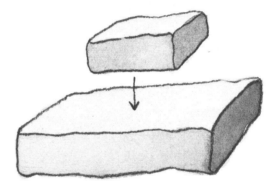

4 Attach four pancake wheels. The top half should stick to the car body and the bottom half should stick out below to hold the car up.

5 Make bumpers out of thin snakes. Add some pancake headlights and pancake hub-caps.

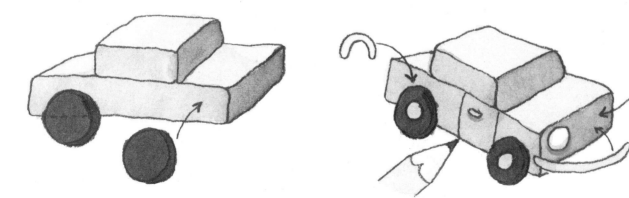

6 Experiment with body shapes to make your favourite cars. Change the wheels' size, add fancy pipes and details and design a car of the past or future.

7 To make a convertible, use a bent paper clip to scoop out the inside of the car, then add a pancake steering wheel.

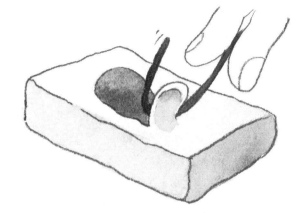

8 Add a windshield and other details and put in some passengers. Make passengers only from the waist up so that they fit in easily.

9 Basic shapes can also be combined to make trains, busses and planes.

49

Sailing, Sailing

Here are a few boat-building ideas in case your Plasticine people find themselves at a lake or the seaside. Anchors aweigh!

1 For a canoe, roll out two thick ribbons and pinch them both into points at the end.

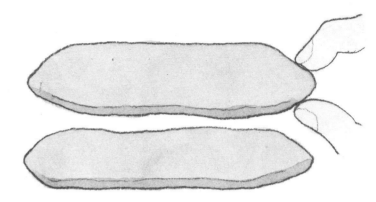

2 Lay the two ribbons side by side so that one overlaps the other slightly. Press them together along the seam.

3 Keeping the seam on the board, fold the sides up. Pinch the ends together. Pinch and mould it into a canoe shape.

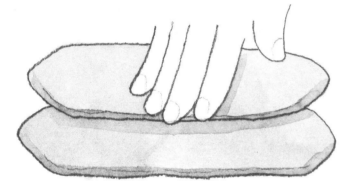

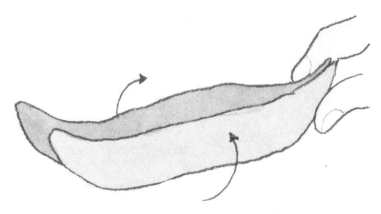

4 To make a seat, lay a short, flat piece of Plasticine across the canoe and pinch it into the sides.

5 A paddle can be made by flattening one end of a snake. Squash the end of the handle to give it a blunt end.

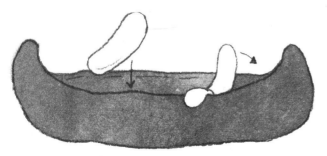

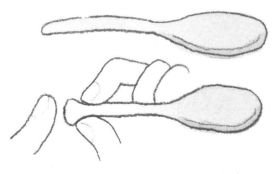

6 To make a row-boat, flatten and pinch a piece of Plasticine into a long triangle. This will be the bottom of the boat.

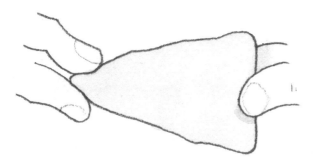

7 Make the sides and back out of ribbons pinched and curved into the right shape.

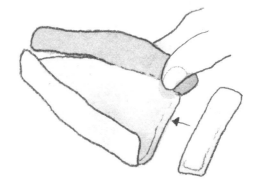

8 You can add seats and even a passenger. Now try some different boat shapes.

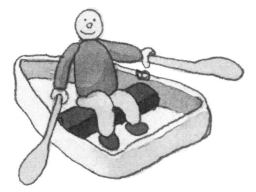

9 A sail can be added by pushing a toothpick through a small square of paper. A small ball of Plasticine on the floor of the boat will hold the sail in place.

10 Try making a fancy speedboat out of a scooped-out egg. Add a water-skier.

11 It's fun to display Plasticine boats on a mirror so that they look as if they're on water. How about making some lily pads — or a sea monster!

Create a Monster

Use some of your favourite Plasticine techniques to make a monster.

1 Once you've created a monster, invent a family for it.

2 What sort of pets would your monster have?

3 Even monsters get tired. What kind of bed would your monster sleep in?

4 Plan a monster picnic. Snail soup? Instant bug breakfast?

5 What would your monster's bathroom look like?

6 If your monster went to school, what would its desk and chair look like?

7 What would its teacher look like?

8 Design a monster-mobile and trailer to take the family camping.

9 Once you create a monster, you'll find there's a whole world of Plasticine to discover. And if your monsters start to take over the house, you can always roll them back up into a lump and wait for them to become something else.

4. Paint a Picture

In this chapter, you'll find out how to "paint" a picture with Plasticine. Instead of a paintbrush, you'll be using your fingers to create pictures and signs with interesting textures. You can create a colourful undersea world, a lumpy, bumpy meadow or an imaginary house you would like to live in. And by adding texture and detail to a flat Plasticine background, you can do things that aren't possible with the three-dimensional figures you've made so far.

TIPS

Cardboard is a great surface on which to make Plasticine pictures. Use cardboard that is stiff enough to hold the Plasticine without flopping over or bending. A slightly rough surface is good; it helps the Plasticine stick. Illustration board, available at art and some craft stores, works very well. The cardboard back of a writing pad or a heavy duty paper plate is a good surface, too.

It's a good idea to plan your picture out on a separate piece of paper. That way, as you work, you can check your plan to make sure you haven't left something out or accidentally covered it over.

Covering the cardboard base of your pictures with a background layer of Plasticine is very important. This layer will stick to the cardboard and provide a sticky surface for other Plasticine details. It's also important to keep the layers of Plasticine fairly thin. Otherwise, large lumps may fall off when you stand your picture up. Layers should be about 0.5 to 1 cm (¼ to ½ inch) thick. Always press details firmly into place.

If you're planning to hang your picture on the wall, you should attach a string or hook to the back *before* you do your picture. That way your picture won't get squashed.

Suppose you make a mistake and some part of your picture isn't the way you wanted it to be. Just peel or scrape off the mistake and re-work it. A small mistake can be covered up with a fresh layer of Plasticine.

Feel free to mix and match texture techniques in this chapter to make your own ideas take shape — so grab a board and start the artwork.

Sky's the Limit

A first layer of Plasticine can become the sky, a heavenly background for some high-flying details.

1 Stick a small lump of softened Plasticine onto the cardboard and spread it by pushing it with your thumb.

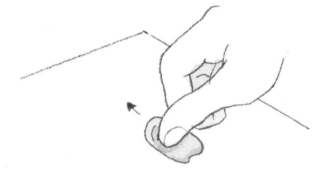

2 Once the first piece is done, add another the same way. It's easiest to push the Plasticine in the direction away from you. Turn the board as you go.

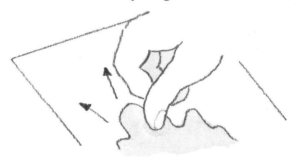

3 If some spots are too thin, add another small lump of Plasticine and blend it in. Bit by bit you will cover the whole area with a thin, even layer of Plasticine.

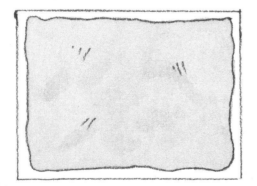

Note: Plasticine pictures are built layer on layer. Try to make the background the farthest thing away from you. For example, the farthest thing away in an outdoor scene may be the sky. Everything else is in front of it. Make it your first layer of Plasticine. Often the most important things in a Plasticine picture are the last things to be added.

4 Once the sky background layer is done, you might want to add a yellow or orange pancake sun.

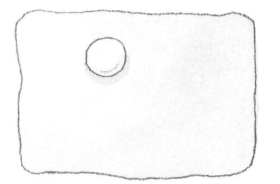

5 Triangle sun-shaped rays can be added. You can even stick on a face.

6 Overlapping a few pancakes of different sizes makes a fluffy cloud.

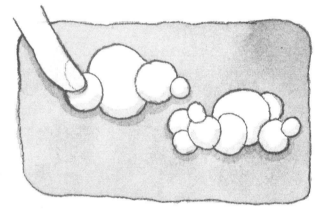

7 Press on small drop shapes to make rain. A zig-zag ribbon becomes lightning.

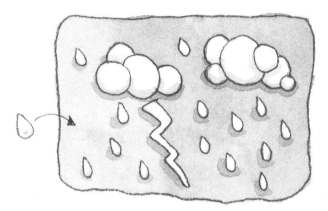

8 The sky can be many colours. For a sunset, try a striped background of pink, orange and purple.

9 Make a night sky with stars and a moon. Or fill the sky with a rainbow after a storm.

Down to Earth

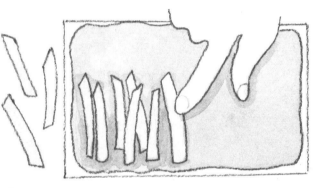

What better background can there be than ground itself! Textures can turn Plasticine into grass, dirt, stones and so on.

1 To make grass, gently scratch a green background with a fork or your fingernail. A small piece of comb works well, too.

2 By cutting thin ribbons or snakes and pressing them down in layers, you can make individual blades of grass.

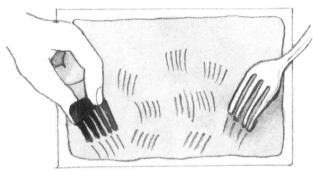

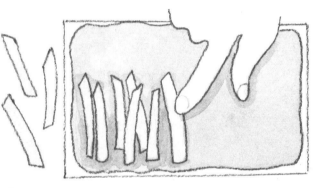

3 To make mud, spread on a thick layer of Plasticine and pinch and prod it with your fingers until it's lumpy. Use pancakes to form clods of dirt or stones.

4 Make a winding road out of a ribbon pressed onto the background. If you're making a sidewalk, scratch pavement lines in with a pencil.

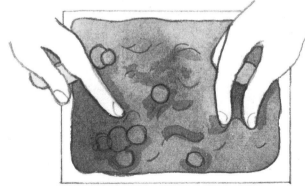

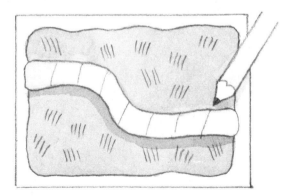

5 To make sandy ground, dot the surface all over with a sharp pencil.

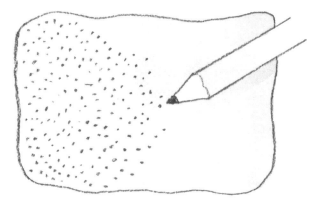

6 Want to make water? Scratch some wavy lines in your background or press on some wiggly snakes to look like ripples.

7 Sometimes you'll want earth *and* sky together in your background. First, figure out how much sky you want to see and spread it onto the board. Spread a little sky into the ground area, too.

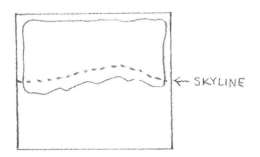

8 To get a smooth skyline, press a ribbon of ground-coloured Plasticine along the skyline. Then smooth it down. Fill in the rest with your thumbs.

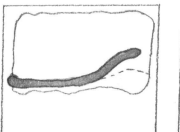 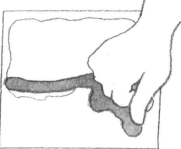

9 One scene can include several types of ground. Experiment with different combinations of sky and earth layers and textures. You can scratch your initials in a Plasticine sidewalk, too.

How Does Your Garden Grow?

Once you've made an earth and sky background, you may want to see what you can grow. Here are some ideas for growing everything from dandelions to exotic trees.

1 Trees and flowers off in the distance don't have to be very detailed. Use pancakes with stems for trees and small balls of colour for flowers.

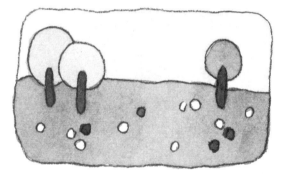

2 To make a more detailed tree, start with a ribbon trunk and blend on some sausage roots and snake branches. Texture the trunk with scratches, bumps or wrinkles made out of tiny snakes.

3 Cover your tree with leaves. These can be bunches of pancakes or layers of flattened triangles. You might add some colourful fruit such as round red apples or cherries. Experiment!

4 To make a fir tree, start with a small ribbon trunk and overlap triangle shapes from bottom to top. Small cuts on the edges will look like needles.

5 Make a cactus out of a flat sausage stem. Add bent sausage branches and cut lines in. Don't forget some dots for prickles.

6 A simple flower has a snake stem, flat pointy leaves and a pancake blossom. Dot the centre of the blossom with a pencil or press in a tiny pancake of a different colour. To make a daisy, cut lines around the edge of the blossom.

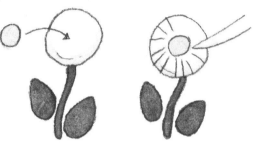

7 For a more detailed flower, put together petals made out of small, flattened sausage petals. If you want, draw veins on the leaves.

8 You can grow a whole rose bush by rolling up thin snakes and adding leaves.

9 Farm fields can be made by scratching rows into the ground with a fork or pencil. Rows of thin snakes look like crops. Try them in different colours.

10 The plants in your Plasticine picture tell the time of year — for example, yellow leaves and bare branches say it's fall. Plants also give your picture a setting — a garden, desert, meadow and so on. Maybe it's a jungle out there!

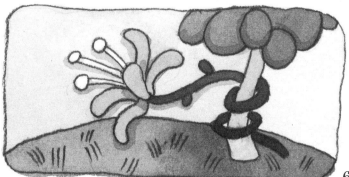

Props and People

Remember how tricky it was to get three-dimensional Plasticine objects to stand up? That's not a problem with flat pictures. You can stick on anything you want and create people who can run, jump, climb and even fly!

1 Stick down a row of flat ribbons for a picket fence. Or make thick snake fenceposts and add skinny snakes to join them for a wire fence. Experiment with fence styles and gates.

2 Tall thin ribbons look like telephone poles if you add some skinny snake wires. Put some stripes onto a pole and turn it into a bus stop.

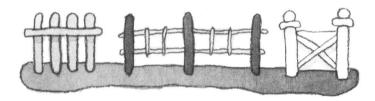

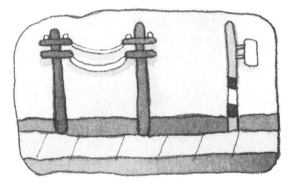

3 If there is a tree in your picture, make a tire swing for it. Curve a thick snake into a doughnut shape and hang it from the tree by a thin snake rope.

4 Draw a hockey net into the background Plasticine with a pencil. Cut in the netting with a knife and make the frame out of thin snakes.

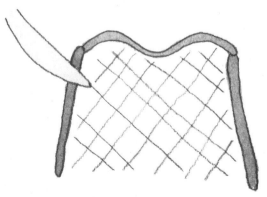

5 Two Xs made of thin snakes make the legs for a picnic table. Press a board made out of a ribbon across the top and another ribbon halfway down for a bench.

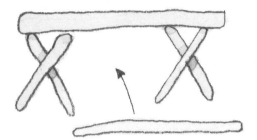

6 Spider webs are fun to make. From a middle point, stick skinny snakes outwards. Press on thin snake cross pieces in a circle. Attach your net to a leaf and add a spider from page 18.

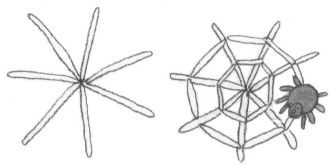

7 Turn a whole herd of thick and thin snakes into a swing set. Try a jungle gym or a slide.

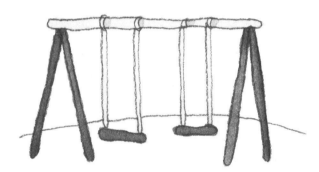

8 Add people to your props. To make sure the figures are the right size, sketch them onto the background with a pencil first. Start with the body and add the limbs.

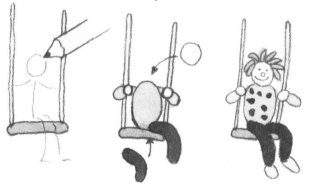

9 Making Plasticine people in pictures is almost the same as making the three-dimensional ones in Part 2. The only difference is that the basic shapes are flat — balls become pancakes, for example.

Plasticine characters can do lots of things when they're in a picture. They can do handstands, skip rope and they never fall off their bicycles.

Home Sweet Home

Plasticine boards and bricks can be pressed into place to build a dog house, your house or even an out house!

1 Sketch the house shape into the Plasticine. To get straight walls, press flat ribbons of Plasticine around the edges before you fill in the inside.

2 Cover your house in pancake-shaped stones (great for a castle) or cut a ribbon into pieces for bricks.

3 Add a roof shingled in overlapping rectangles of ribbon. Start at the bottom and work up. Make a thatched roof by scratching in a straw texture or adding layers of snakes.

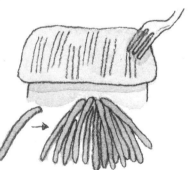

4 Doors can be outlined and filled in or shaped in your fingers and stuck on. To make a wooden door, line up strips of ribbon. Round balls make good door knobs.

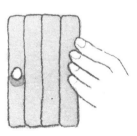

5 Experiment with window shapes and sizes. Thin snakes can be criss-crossed to make panes, flat ribbons can make window ledges or sills and you can even add a flower box.

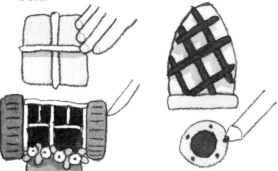

6 Press on layers of overlapping ribbons to make a wooden house. Start at the bottom and work up. Some boards can join partway across. Pencil dots look like nails.

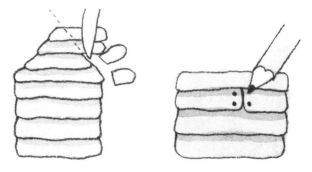

7 A door or window can be cut in a wooden house. Then carefully peel off or scrape out the boards. Fill in the inside. Maybe there's something in there.

8 You can even make an igloo. Roll out a thin flat piece of Plasticine (make sure it doesn't stick to the table) and cut out blocks of snow.

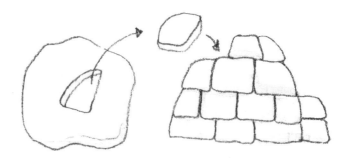

9 Combine shapes and textures to make all sorts of houses and buildings. Keep them plain or decorate them into something fancy.

Make buildings you've seen as well as some you'd like to see.

The Great Indoors

What did Goldilocks see when she peeked in the door of the three bears' house? You can make the three bears' furniture and whole house out of Plasticine.

1 The bears might have had walls of just one colour, but you can create wallpaper by adding snake stripes, polka dots or tiny flowers.

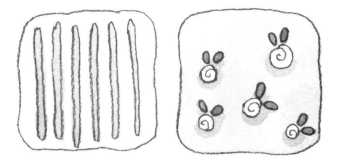

2 Draw a window on the wall and scrape out what's inside. Fill the space with some sky and whatever else you might see out the window. Frame and divide the window into panes with snakes and add curtains or a blind.

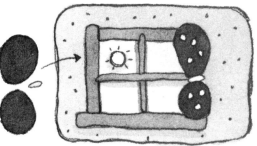

3 Decorate the walls of the bears' house with pictures, or press a pancake onto the wall and add dots and snakes to make a clock.

4 To make a wooden floor, press flat ribbons down side by side. Remember, they'll stick better if there's already a layer of Plasticine on the board. Dot on some nail holes.

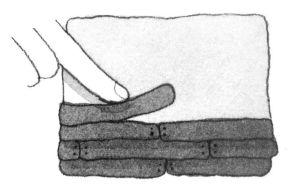

5 You can make a checkered floor by cutting different coloured ribbons into squares and alternating them. Or press some mixed-up marbled Plasticine onto the floor.

6 Use lots of different shapes to make furniture — a chair that's too hard, one that's too soft and one just right.

7 Try making a kitchen scene with a table and dishes. Some long wavy snakes will look like steam rising from a bowl of porridge that's too hot.

8 Coil up some multicoloured snakes to make a bedroom rug. To make Goldilocks in bed, make the bed, then the part of the body that sticks out of the bed, then the covers. Try making a colourful quilt.

9 There are hundreds of other indoor scenes that can be made out of Plasticine. You could show dark, rough walls inside a bat cave, sandy tunnels in an anthill or the inside of a bakery with lots of pies, cakes and cookies.

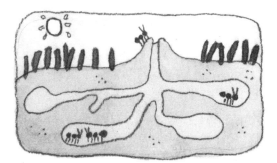

67

Something Fishy

It's fun to make an underwater scene with Plasticine. Because the figures are pressed onto a background, they can look as if they're floating anywhere in the scene. And you can make some thin, delicate shapes too.

1 Start your underwater scene with a smooth background. You can use a solid colour or a mixture of blues, greens and purples for a wavy, watery look.

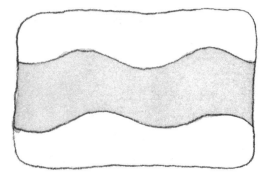

2 A simple fish starts with a flat drop shape and gets a bent sausage mouth. Add an eye, fins and a tail. You can even add scales, if you want.

3 Experiment with different fish shapes. You can make fish that are found in aquariums or imaginary undersea creatures. Use lots of colours. Marbled Plasticine looks great on tropical fish.

4 Press long snakes and leaf shapes onto the background to form underwater plants.

5 To make a starfish, start with a round ball and pinch out five points. Press it onto the board and add a texture. Don't forget seashells and snails.

6 To make an octopus, start with an oval body and add eight snake legs. Suction cups are easy. Press thin pancakes on and dot with a pencil.

7 You can add scuba divers, too. Start with a body, add arms, legs, head, a cylinder tank and triangle flippers. A diver can "swim" all over the picture.

8 If the background of your picture is made of water and sky, you can show a whale leaping out of the water or spouting.

9 Try different bottom textures, such as sand and rocks. Imagine what you might see if you were exploring the sea or a lake you know.

Far Out!

Let your imagination zoom into space to make some really out-of-this-world pictures.

1 Start with a dark background and add bright little dots of Plasticine for faraway stars. This will give your picture an outer-space feeling. Try some constellations.

2 To make a streaking comet, start with a small bit of bright colour. Press it onto the background with your thumb and smear it across the sky to form the comet's tail. Add a small ball of bright colour to the head of the comet.

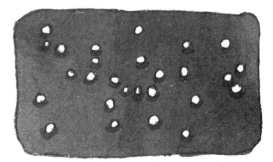

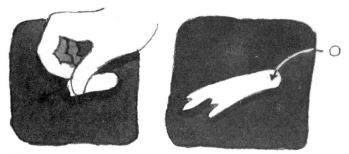

3 Make planets out of different sizes of pancakes. For a really big planet, press on a ribbon outline and fill it in. Planets may be marbled, striped or have rings around them.

4 Make craters by pressing with round objects, such as pencil points and erasers. It's a good idea to make your planets thick [up to ¼ inch], so that the craters don't go right through the board underneath.

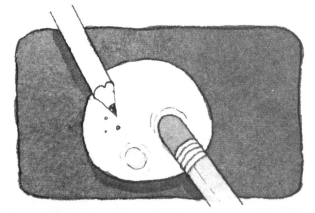

5 To make a big crater, start with a thick snake and press it onto the planet in a doughnut shape. Smooth the outer edge into the background. Scratch some rough spots in with a pencil.

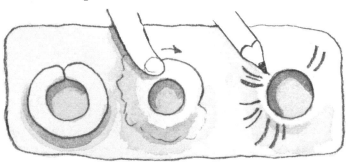

6 You can also put pointed mountains on your planet or try a bubbling lava lake.

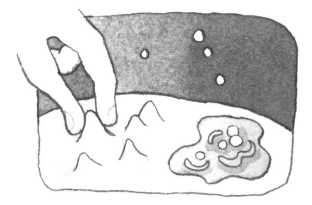

7 Combine cylinders, pancakes and dots to make rockets and spacecraft.

8 Bright drop shapes can be pressed on to look like rocket engine flames. Pancakes make a cloud of smoke. And long, thin snakes look like laser beams or jet streams.

9 Don't forget astronauts joined to their ships by long snakes or zipping along on jet scooters. They might even meet some alien life forms from distant galaxies.

A Bird's Eye View

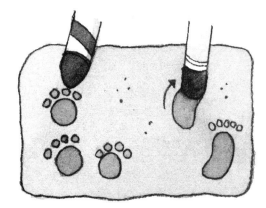

Have you ever stood on a ladder and looked straight down, or looked out of an aircraft window to the land below? Using Plasticine, you can make some unusual pictures from this "bird's eye view."

1 If you were gliding in the sky above a beach, you'd see lots of sand. To make sand for your picture, spread the Plasticine fairly thickly [about ¼ inch] so that it can be textured easily. Then start dotting.

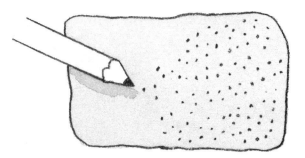

2 Use different sized objects to press footprints into the sand. Try a pencil eraser or a crayon point.

3 Spread a beach towel on the sand. Outline the towel and fill it in, or make it up with stripes or flat ribbons.

4 Stretch a person on the towel. Start with the body and add arms, legs and head.

5 Maybe your person is buried in the sand. Cover the body with a layer of sand-coloured Plasticine and leave the head and toes sticking out.

6 To make a beach umbrella seen from the air, draw a circle on the sand and fit in some long triangles. Add a ball in the middle.

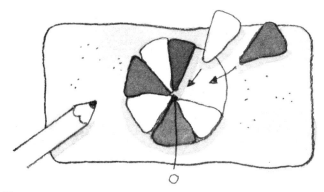

7 If someone was under this umbrella, from the air all you'd see would be toes sticking out.

8 To make someone floating on water, start with a blue background. Press on body parts that are out of the water and some snake ripples.

9 Experiment with different surfaces. Try looking down on someone reading comics on the floor. What about someone making an angel in the snow? You can make tracks in the snow, too. Bird's eye pictures take a bit of thinking and planning, but they're the next best thing to flying.

LOSE YOUR TURN

GO BACK

JASON'S ROOM

5. For Keeps

It's often fun to squish up your Plasticine creations and make something new. But this chapter offers some suggestions for things you might like to keep for a while or give as gifts.

TIPS

Plasticine always stays soft, no matter how long it's been around. That can cause a problem if you want to keep your Plasticine creations. They may get squashed or fall apart from handling.

To preserve three-dimensional objects, store them in plastic tubs or anchor them firmly to a solid cardboard base so that they can be picked up without being squashed.

Flat pictures are easier to preserve because everything is pressed firmly onto a cardboard base. You can hang flat Plasticine pictures on a wall out of harm's way or keep them flat in a box. To keep them clean, cover them lightly with plastic wrap or waxed paper. You can stack up several Plasticine pictures if there's a layer of waxed paper between them.

Easy as A, B, C

Shaping letters out of Plasticine will let you add words to your pictures or make a sign for your bedroom wall.

1 To make simple letters, roll out a long thin snake. Cut off a piece that will form the main part of the letter, for example, the straight part in the letter R.

2 Press the first part of the letter onto a Plasticine background. Cut out pieces to form the rest of the letter and stick them on.

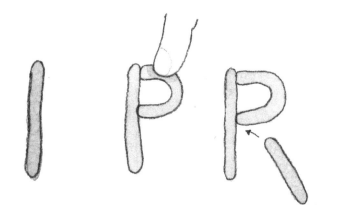

3 You can use snakes to print words in lots of colours, shapes and sizes.

4 Long snakes can also be used for writing, just as you would with a pen. It might take several snakes to do a whole word. Just smooth the joins with your fingers.

5 Flat ribbons can be cut to form fat block letters. You can make fancy letters by twisting two snakes together.

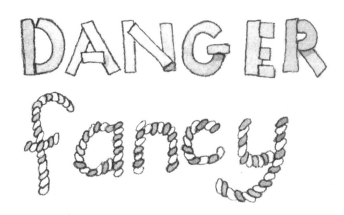

6 To make a sign in Plasticine, attach strings or a hook to the back of a piece of cardboard so that it can be hung up.

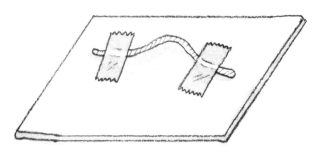

7 Cover the board with a thin layer of Plasticine (for tips on how to do this, see page 56). If you want your lettering straight, lay a ruler down and scratch a faint line on the Plasticine.

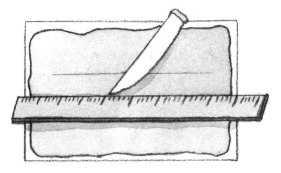

8 On a piece of paper the same size as your sign, write or print the name you want to make. Using this as your guide, stick down the letters.

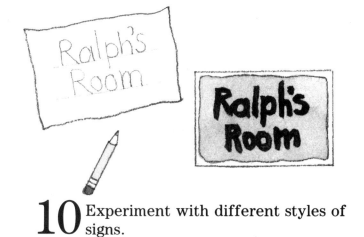

9 You can decorate your sign with other Plasticine stuff. Just make sure everything is pressed *firmly* so that pieces won't fall off when it's hung.

10 Experiment with different styles of signs.

Express Yourself

Many artists use themselves as models to create self-portraits. There's a self-portrait of me on the back of this book. Why not use Plasticine to capture the real you?

1 Cut a piece of cardboard to the size you want. It's easier to work with small areas — 5 x 7 inches is ideal.

2 If you want to be able to hang your picture, punch a small hole near the top of the cardboard with the pointed end of scissors or a nail. Ask an adult to help you with this. Later you can thread a string through.

3 To make a picture stand up, cut a triangle out of stiff, thin cardboard or bristol board. Fold it along one edge as shown.

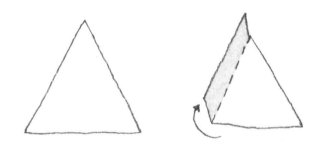

4 Tape the folded edge of the triangle to the back of the piece of cardboard near the bottom. The triangle will stick out and hold up the board.

5 The triangle can be folded flat against the back as you work.

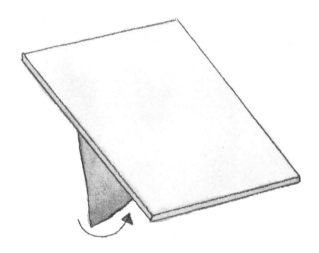

6 Cover the whole front of the board with a background layer of Plasticine, then scratch in the outline of your head, neck and shoulders. Look in a mirror or use a photo to help you.

7 Outline and fill in this area with flesh-coloured Plasticine, and add a nose and ears. Press on white eyes with the right colour of pupils and a red mouth. Look carefully at your features as you work.

8 Hair can be made using snakes, scratching on a texture or piling up pancakes. Don't forget details such as freckles, moles, braces or dimples that make you special. Add your favourite shirt.

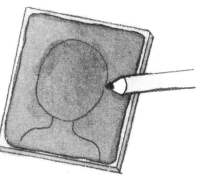

9 Make a Plasticine frame for your picture using thin or thick snakes, or decorate it with squiggles and flowers. You can give your portrait to someone as a gift.

10 Make portraits of your family. Experiment with different sizes and shapes. Soon your wall or desk can become a portrait gallery! You can write on your portraits, too.

Fun & Games

Make up your own board game and invite your friends over to play with Plasticine in more ways than one.

1 You'll need a large piece of heavy cardboard about the size of two pages in this book. Cover it with a layer of Plasticine.

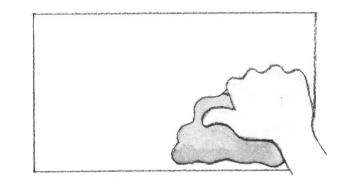

2 Draw a twisty trail onto the board with a pencil. This will be the path the players must follow.

3 Write the word "Start" at one end and "Finish" at the other.

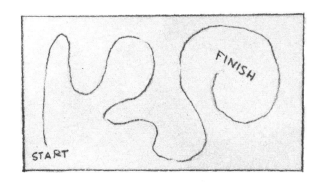

4 Make a long, thick snake and use a pencil to roll it into a ribbon about ¾ inch wide.

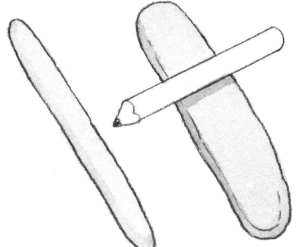

5 Cut the ribbon into squares. Press these squares onto the path. You'll need lots of squares of different colours, depending on the rules of your game.

6 Make up rules. Here's an example:

To play, players roll one die and move ahead the number they roll. If they land on a coloured square, they have to follow the instructions for that colour. For example:

> red square — roll again
> blue — move ahead two squares
> orange — go back four squares
> yellow — miss a turn

You might even have a polka dot square that means a player must sing a song, or a striped one that means all players change seats. Have fun thinking up your rules.

7 Instead of using buttons or coins as markers, make your own Plasticine characters to move around the board. They can be animals, people or objects. Attach each one to a solid Plasticine base so that they will stand up and be easy to move.

Between games, cover your board with plastic wrap or waxed paper and store your markers in Styrofoam egg cartons. That way your game will stay clean until next time. For more ideas, turn the page.

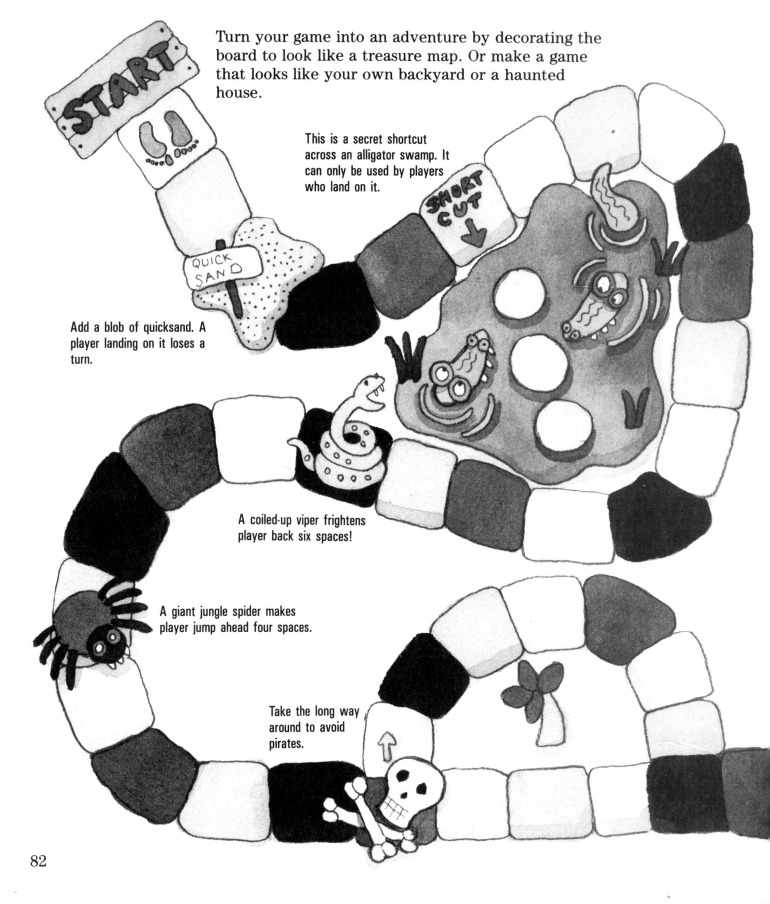

Turn your game into an adventure by decorating the board to look like a treasure map. Or make a game that looks like your own backyard or a haunted house.

This is a secret shortcut across an alligator swamp. It can only be used by players who land on it.

Add a blob of quicksand. A player landing on it loses a turn.

A coiled-up viper frightens player back six spaces!

A giant jungle spider makes player jump ahead four spaces.

Take the long way around to avoid pirates.

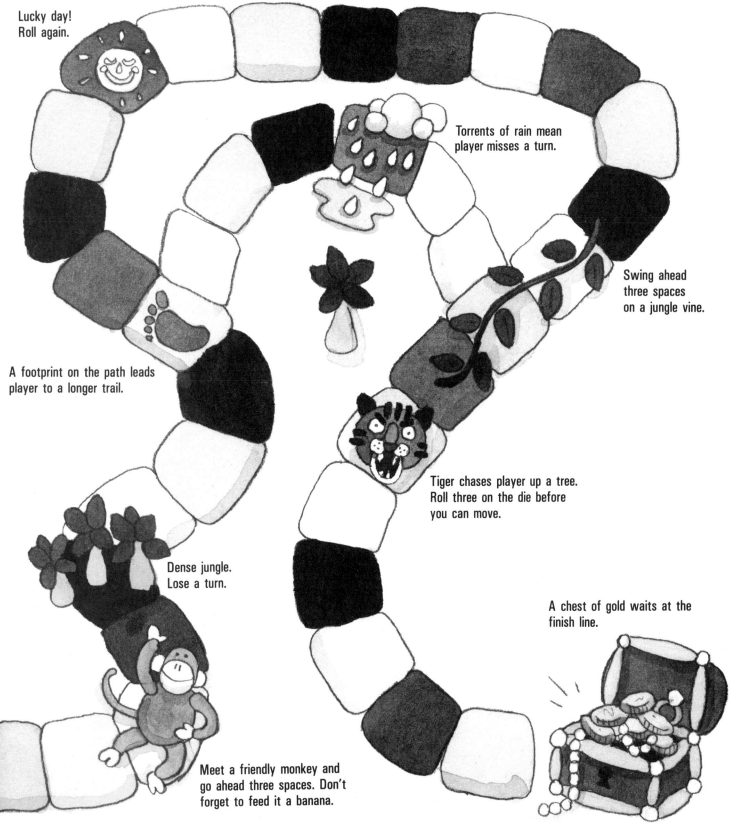

Lucky day! Roll again.

Torrents of rain mean player misses a turn.

Swing ahead three spaces on a jungle vine.

A footprint on the path leads player to a longer trail.

Tiger chases player up a tree. Roll three on the die before you can move.

Dense jungle. Lose a turn.

A chest of gold waits at the finish line.

Meet a friendly monkey and go ahead three spaces. Don't forget to feed it a banana.

6. Special Effects

Wouldn't some of your three-dimensional Plasticine figures and animals look great with a Plasticine backdrop? In this chapter, you'll find out how to get some really special effects by combining three-dimensional figures and flat pictures. You'll also have a chance to mix and match the Plasticine techniques you've played with so far to create exciting illustrations, theatre sets and models. You'll even learn how to turn packages, cups and other stuff into Plasticine scenes. The special effects in this chapter take more time and planning than any you've done so far, but the results are worth the extra effort.

TIPS

Read the instructions all the way through before you begin a project. Plan your project and make sure you have all the materials you need. Some of these projects use quite a lot of Plasticine, as well as objects such as milk cartons, yogurt containers, scissors and tape.

When you're using something as a base — for example, a yogurt container — make sure Plasticine will stick to it before you tape it into place. Plasticine doesn't stick well to Styrofoam, but it really gloms onto most plastic, metal and cardboard.

Some projects require taping. Be sure to do *all* the taping before you touch any Plasticine. If you don't, the oil in the Plasticine will prevent the tape from sticking.

It might take two or three sittings to make a whole play or dinosaur world. Once the basic construction is done, flip back through the book for reminders on how to finish the project with lots of decoration, texture and detail. As with all Plasticine work, you can change your mind and reshape things any time you wish.

Setting the Scene

Combine flat picture backgrounds with three-dimensional characters and you can bring to life your favourite book, play or movie.

1 A shoe box makes a good set. Lay the box flat and cut out one of the long sides.

2 Turn the box over so that it looks like this and cut a triangle from each side. Now you have a sturdy, stand-up background.

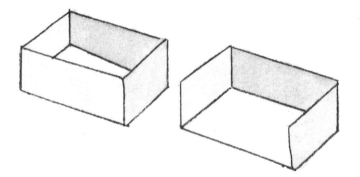

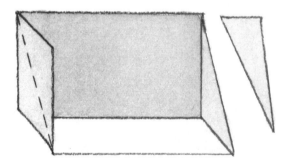

3 Let's say you decided to put on a play, Hansel and Gretel. Lay your box on its back so that it's easier to work on.

4 Cover the back with a layer of Plasticine and make a flat picture as you did in Part 4.

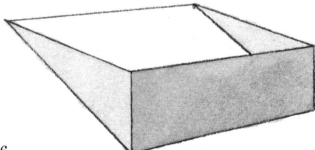

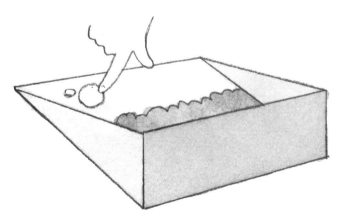

5 If you're making the gingerbread house, make lots of colourful Plasticine cookies, candies and icing. Press them on firmly.

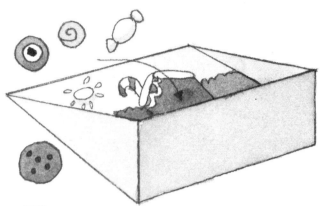

6 Set your box upright again and make a grass floor by adding a layer of green Plasticine. Put in your figures of Hansel and Gretel. What about the birds that ate their bread trail?

7 Once you've finished the outside, make the inside of the witch's house. Add some spider webs to make the place look spooky and a wooden floor like the one in number 4, page 66.

8 Time to add the witch. Make her nose out of a skinny triangle and add a few bumps. Don't forget a black cat.

9 If you make several box sets in a row, you can tell a whole story. Or make several rooms in the same house and put different characters in each. You can even

make movable backdrops out of cardboard and insert them into your box frame to change scenes.

Cover Up!

Turn garbage into art! Plasticine coverings can transform lots of empty containers and packages into model buildings and much more.

1 Start with a cardboard base. A shallow box lid works well because it helps contain all the objects in your landscape.

2 Find a container or other object that is the right shape for what you want to make. Small tin cans and boxes, yogurt containers and bottle tops all have interesting shapes.

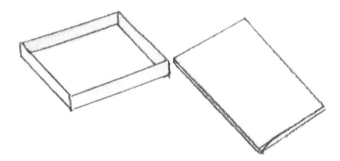

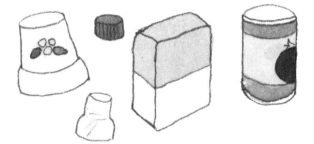

3 You can also use cardboard milk cartons or paper cups. Stuff these firmly with scrunched up newspaper so that they're strong. Plasticine won't stick to Styrofoam, so don't use Styrofoam cups or plates.

4 A milk carton is shaped like a house. You can cut off the top ridge and tape it shut.

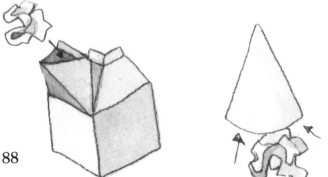

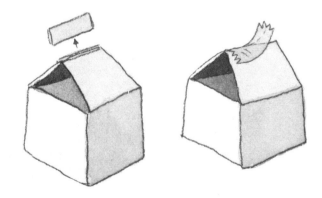

5 Firmly tape the milk carton or other object into position on the board. If you want several objects on the board, do *all* the taping before you start to add any Plasticine.

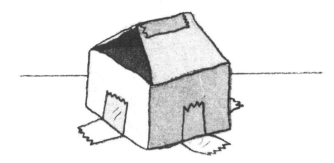

6 Carefully spread a base layer of Plasticine over the object. Work with small, flattened pieces of very soft Plasticine. Smooth pieces into place.

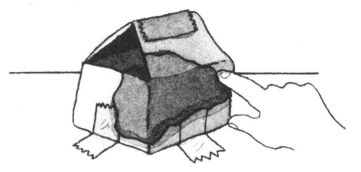

7 Once the object is covered, you can stick on details. For a house, stick on boards, a chimney, shingles, windows and so on. See pages 64-65 for ideas.

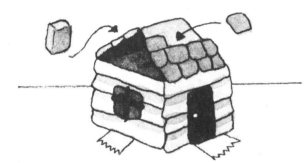

8 Spread Plasticine over the base of your landscape and add textures and shapes to finish off your scene.

9 See what you can recycle from around your home to create rocket launch pads, farm scenes or city scapes.

King of the Castle

If you're interested in castles, knights, dragons and sorcerers, why not make your own? Start by drawing your scene, then get out the Plasticine.

1 Securely tape a small yogurt cup or tin can to a cardboard base. Use a flat piece of cardboard or a shoe-box lid.

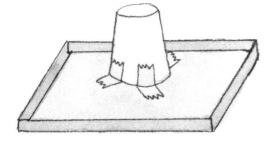

2 Carefully press on a base layer of Plasticine all over the cup. Draw on lines to look like bricks or cover your tower with bricks made from a flat ribbon of Plasticine.

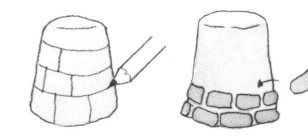

3 Make a thick snake and flatten it with a roller. Cut this into blocks for the top of the tower. Leave some spaces between blocks.

4 With a sharp pencil, press arrow slits into the tower sides. You might even add a small door at the bottom with heavy bolts and hinges.

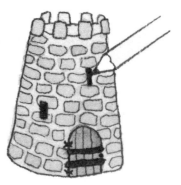

5 If yours is an enchanted tower, add a magician to the top, casting a spell or watching for approaching travellers.

6 With more Plasticine, you can make the tower in the middle of a grassy meadow or a stony plain. Use ribbons of Plasticine joined together to make a winding path.

7 To make a stream or moat, outline and then fill in the water areas. You can get a clear edge between the water and shore by pressing a thick land-coloured snake along the water's edge. Smooth it away from the water.

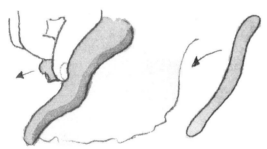

8 Add a drawbridge to your tower. Real twigs can serve as trees.

9 Try a scene with more than one tower, or use tape and cardboard to make walls between two towers to make a whole castle. Just remember to do *all* taping before you put on any Plasticine.

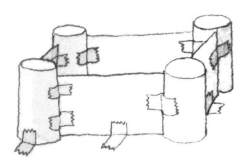

10 Have fun adding a whole cast of characters and animals to your castle. And don't forget a dragon!

Dinosaur Days

Recreate the age of the dinosaurs with some yogurt cups, imagination and Plasticine know-how.

1 Start with a shallow box lid or piece of cardboard. Stuff pointed paper cups with newspaper to make them solid and securely tape them to the board to make a mountain range.

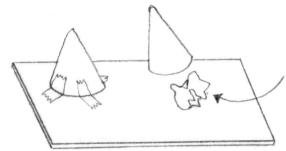

2 Trim off the base of one cup to make a smaller mountain. Tape down a yogurt cup with sloping sides to make a volcano.

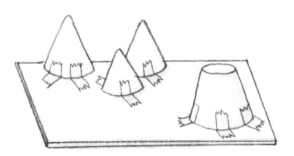

3 To make a lake, tape a small mirror or piece of aluminum foil onto the board. The tape at the edges won't show when the Plasticine goes on.

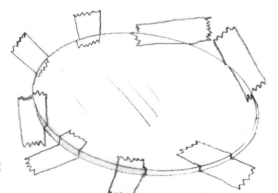

4 Cover the mountains and ground with a base layer of Plasticine. The mountains may be grey or black or bright prehistoric colours. Work slowly with small, flat pieces of very soft Plasticine. Smooth the base of each mountain into the ground.

5 Press a thick, land-coloured snake around the lake to form a shoreline and smooth it into the ground. You might make a rough and rocky texture around the mountains that changes to a greener, grassy area near the lake.

6 Use a thick snake to form a rim around the volcano. To make it erupt, mix up red and orange Plasticine to look like marbly lava. Roll out lava snakes and press them on.

7 Add on some small balls to look like bubbling lava. To make a puff of smoke, stretch out a small bit of cotton batting. Use a pencil to poke one end of it into the Plasticine at the top of the volcano.

8 Make some prehistoric plants, especially around the lake. To help the trees stand up, give them a good solid base and gently insert a bit of toothpick into them.

9 Don't forget the dinosaurs! Try them in all sorts of shapes and colours. They can be rising out of the lake, eating a tree or running from the volcano and each other.

And don't stop with dinosaur days. There are many more worlds to create. How about a treasure island, the Antarctic, the pyramids or....

PLASTICINE THEN AND NOW

You may have heard the story of how the telephone was invented or even the airplane. But what about Plasticine? How was it invented?

Like many inventions, Plasticine was the solution to a problem. A hundred years ago an art teacher in England named William Harbutt became frustrated with clay. It was heavy and difficult for his students to use. So William Harbutt began experimenting to see if he could come up with something better.

He mixed batches of stuff together in his basement until, one day in about 1887, he produced a soft, light-weight, easy-to-handle material which he called Plasticine. His students loved the stuff. And so did his six children. That started Harbutt thinking. If *his* children enjoyed Plasticine so much, maybe other children would, too. So he started to advertise it in magazines with this catchy slogan:

Plasticine is something new
And hopes to make a friend of you.

The Harbutts were swamped with orders. To meet the demand, William Harbutt hired an old soldier who mixed the ingredients by hand and flattened big batches with a heavy garden roller.

Over the years, Plasticine has been used by adults as well as children. During the Second World War, Plasticine models were made of enemy territory. Army commanders studied these models before planning attacks. More recently Plasticine models of cars and buildings have been placed in wind tunnels to see how wind flows over and around them. And the world's first spacesuit was modelled in — you guessed it! — Plasticine before the real version was made.

Today's Plasticine is more colourful than the first Plasticine (it came in only one colour — grey), but otherwise it looks just like the stuff William Harbutt made in his basement. The recipe for making Plasticine has stayed the same, too. It's made from a mixture of petroleum jelly, lard, limestone, colouring and...a secret ingredient that no one will reveal. Hmmm...what do *you* think that secret ingredient might be?